Wildlife of the Great Basin

Cristina Bochenski

ROSEN
COMMON CORE
READERS

Rosen
Classroom™

New York

Published in 2014 by The Rosen Publishing Group, Inc.
29 East 21st Street, New York, NY 10010

Book Design: Jon D'Rozario

Photo Credits: Cover Darren J. Bradley/Shutterstock.com; pp. 3, 4, 6, 8, 10, 12, 14, 16, 18, 20, 22, 23, 24 (background) Leigh Prather/Shutterstock.com; p. 5 (map) Dr_Flash/Shutterstock.com; p. 5 (desert) Kobby Dagan/Shutterstock.com; p. 7 Dave Rock/Shutterstock.com; p. 9 Melissa E Dockstader/Shutterstock.com; p. 11 mikenorton/Shutterstock.com; p. 13 visuelldesign/Shutterstock.com; p. 15 Joe Farah/Shutterstock.com; p. 17 Nate Allred/Shutterstock.com; p. 19 (badger) Max Allen/Shutterstock.com; p. 19 (rat) C. Allan Morgan/Peter Arnold/Getty Images; p. 21 (coyote) Terje Langeland/Shutterstock.com; p. 21 (mountain lion) Ronnie Howard/Shutterstock.com.

ISBN: 978-1-4777-2476-7
6-pack ISBN: 978-1-4777-2477-4

Manufactured in the United States of America

CPSIA Compliance Information: Batch #CS13RC: For further information contact Rosen Publishing, New York, New York at 1-800-237-9932.

Contents

Great Basin Basics

The Great Basin is a huge area of dry land in the western United States. Its biggest, most famous feature is the Great Basin Desert. The desert takes up around 190,000 square miles (492,000 sq km) and covers parts of Nevada, California, Idaho, Oregon, and Utah. Two mountain ranges mark the edges of the Great Basin: the Sierra Nevada on the west and the Rocky Mountains on the east.

The Great Basin Desert is the largest of the four U.S. deserts. The others are the Sonoran (suh-NOHR-uhn), Chihuahuan (chee-WAH-wahn), and Mojave (moh-HAH-vee).

The Great Basin Desert is home to many kinds of plants and animals. They're able to live and grow in the desert's dry weather.

Great Basin

What's an Adaptation?

The Sierra Nevada are so tall they keep rain from reaching the Great Basin Desert. Only 6 to 12 inches (15 to 30 cm) of **precipitation** fall there each year. The Great Basin Desert is cold, not hot, because it's at a high **elevation**.

Because of the cold, dry weather, plants and animals have adaptations (aa-dap-TAY-shunz) that allow them to live there. Adaptations are body parts or ways of life that form over time to help plants and animals stay alive.

Some parts of the Great Basin are so cold it snows! ▶

Great Basin Desert Plants

Over 800 **species** of plants can be found in the Great Basin Desert! These plants have adaptations that help them get water from the **environment** and hold on to it for a long time.

Big sagebrush is one of the most common plants in the Great Basin Desert. Its leaves are hairy to keep the wind from drying them out. The roots of a big sagebrush spread out far under the ground to get as much water as possible.

The big sagebrush's adaptations allow it to grow all over the Great Basin Desert.

9

The Great Basin Desert is also home to many kinds of trees, such as firs, willows, and oaks. It's also home to different kinds of pine trees. The Great Basin bristlecone pine is the longest-living tree on Earth. These trees have been known to live for almost 5,000 years!

Bristlecone pine trees have needles that can last for more than 40 years. They grow very slowly. This makes them great trees for a desert because it's too dry for trees to grow quickly.

Bristlecone pine trees grow in rocky soil, which allows them to grow strong in a desert.

11

Scary Snakes

Many animals make their homes in the Great Basin Desert and have adapted to life there. Snakes are a common sight in the Great Basin Desert. One of the most famous snakes in this area is the Great Basin rattlesnake. It's light brown or gray, which helps it hide from other animals. Its teeth, or fangs, can force **venom** into other animals and kill them.

Rattlesnakes shake their tail to make a rattling noise to warn predators, such as hawks, to stay away. They eat smaller animals, such as birds, lizards, and mice.

Rattlesnakes wait for their prey to come to them. They can feel the movement of other animals through the ground.

The Life of a Lizard

Lizards are common animals in the Great Basin Desert, too. The Great Basin collared lizard makes its home on the rocky ground. It's known for the two black collars, or rings, around its neck. These lizards have a white band around their neck, too. Great Basin collared lizards can run on two legs instead of four, but only when they're running very fast! They run to chase their prey, which are often other lizards and bugs.

The back legs of a Great Basin collared lizard are very strong. It uses these legs to run.

Spiders and Scorpions

The Great Basin Desert is home to a large number of bugs. Spiders can be easily spotted in the Great Basin Desert by their eight legs and lack of **antennae** or wings. Scorpions are much like spiders, but they have a stinger. A scorpion's stinger can hurt! Scorpions are nocturnal, which means they're most active at night. This is when they hunt spiders and other bugs. Scorpions sting quickly when they're bothered, so it's important to be careful around these creatures.

Some people are very afraid of scorpions, but they rarely sting people.

Mighty Mammals

There are many different mammals living in the Great Basin Desert. Each one has special adaptations to help it stay alive in the desert. Badgers are small but skilled hunters that like to eat rattlesnakes! The snake's venom doesn't hurt them unless they're bitten on the nose.

Kangaroo rats have tan and white fur and a long tail. They store their food in cool, wet places. This allows them to go their whole lives without ever drinking water! That's an important adaptation for a desert animal.

A mammal is an animal with warm blood and fur or hair. These animals drink milk from their mother when they're babies, too.

kangaroo rat

badger

Coyotes can be found in many areas, but they're especially common in the desert. They look much like a dog with gray and red fur. Coyotes can travel more than 400 miles (644 km) to find food, and they will eat nearly anything.

Mountain lions are large cats that hunt deer and elk. They can weigh up to 250 pounds (114 kg) and can drag things that weigh up to three times as much as they do. Mountain lions are able to jump very far to catch their prey!

Coyotes and mountain lions are two common predators in the Great Basin Desert.

coyote

mountain lion

Life in the Desert

Plants and animals in the Great Basin Desert have important adaptations to live in this area. Here are some of the most common examples.

species	adaptations
big sagebrush	hairy leaves, deep and far-reaching roots
Great Basin bristlecone pine	grows slowly in rocky soil
Great Basin rattlesnake	brown and gray skin to blend in with the ground
scorpion	nocturnal to stay out of the heat during the day
badger	able to eat rattlesnakes and not get hurt by venom
kangaroo rat	can go its whole life without drinking water

Glossary

antennae (an-TEH-nee) Long, thin body parts that stick out of an insect's head and are used for sensing. The singular form is "antenna."

elevation (eh-luh-VAY-shun) Height above sea level.

environment (ihn-VY-ruhn-muhnt) The natural world around us.

precipitation (prih-sih-puh-TAY-shun) Moisture that falls from the sky, including rain, snow, and ice.

species (SPEE-sheez) A group of living things that are all of the same kind.

venom (VEH-nuhm) A poison produced by some animals.

Index